The

Ghost

Of

Me

By

Roger Harrison

(c)2022

My depression is layering on top of me more and more until I feel like I can no longer breathe. My past catches up with me like a ghost rider on a pale horse overtaking me. The only light I had has melted away like a candle that will never burn again. For you see I feel my future lies buried in my past that over shadows my present. I do not know how much longer I can live in this plastic world made up of plastic people as my plastic dreams start to melt away into insomniac nightmares. In the world I must exist in I keep trying to hide like a ghost in the walls. From this state of depression is where I wrote these poems.

The Ghost Of Me

Last night I took a walk subconsciously

Glanced in a mirror and saw the ghost of me

I decided that I should start to scream

I was caught between reality and a dream

My ears went deaf and my eyes went blind

When I looked through the prisms of my mind

My sanity left me as my pain did abound

As I tried to walk upon the shaky ground

I could see right through myself to my soul

I saw and felt how life had taken its toll

All my dreams and hopes had faded away

Slowly taken by the passing of each day

Until they were pieces of a forgotten memory

Translucent ramblings of the ghost of me

<u>My Blood</u>

I slice my wrist to watch myself bleed

On my blood my pain it does feed

I watch every drop as it hits the floor

Tell myself I will do this no more

I know to myself that I have lied

As my cells lethargically commit genocide

Like a runaway horse my past catches me

Condemning my future to an inferiority

I try unsuccessfully to wash myself clean

With my blood from pain that is unseen

Pain pulls the strings within my brain

As my blood it likes to systematically drain

My body has become desensitized

I no longer feel the tears that I cry

Tell myself one more time over and over again

My blood will spill until its very end

<u>**Her Memory Remains**</u>

She left me a long time ago

But her memory still remains

I hear her voice in the wind

The sound of her loving refrains

When the cold comes creeping

She is not here to keep me warm

Her memory cannot mend me

Or fix a heart that is torn

We use to be so happy together

We use to be two that were one

Then you took away your love

Then you took away my Sun

I dine alone now every meal

Can no longer get out of bed

See no one or hear their sound

Only echoes of love words you said

She left me a long time ago

But her memory still remains

I hear her voice in the wind

The sound of her loving refrains

<u>Same</u>

I take a walk among the trees

I drop down upon my knees

I pray for a change

Everything remains the same

Different person, different name

Always the same old pain

Starts out with an ethereal Sun

Then the dark clouds come

It always starts to rain

My light has melted into dark

Overshadowed by a broken heart

Happiness I can no longer feign

The fog thick starts its roll in

I am lost in my mind again

Tethered to my fascistic brain

<u>My Misery</u>

There is a misery living in my head

I think that I will just go to bed

Just going to sleep the night away

Then I will sleep the rest of the day

There are idiots and there are fools

They like to use me as their tool

They point at me and laugh at me

They find pleasure in my misery

I could explain but what would I say

They would not understand anyway

Guess it is my own fault to a certain degree

So I will just go on living with my misery

Ruthless

I am ruthless so stay away from me

I want to live in a world that is people free

When I was young everyone said I was nice

Now my heart has turned into shards of ice

Do not come around with your words of love

They choke me like poison on a velvet glove

I cannot be tamed so do not you even try

I will be the way I am until the day I die

Corner Grave

Want you bury me in a corner grave

It is to late now for me to be saved

Cover me with dirt to keep me warm

Like a mother does a baby not yet born

Some will say that it is never to late

They have never had to carry my wait

If you visit me do it only at night time

Cannot stand to see the light I could never find

Do not bring flowers I can no longer smell

I was done in by just one single shell

So please bury me in a corner grave

Do not cry for a man who could not be saved

<h1 style="text-align:center"><u>Seems</u></h1>

Life is not always the way that it seems

Sometimes a nightmare is your only dream

People see your smile and think all is fine

They cannot see the pain that is in your mind

They think that you are riding so very high

They cannot see the hurt in you that you cry

You have no right to be sad they will say

They have never lived a life through your day

Stalked by your deepest of dark fears

Feeding off every drop of every single tear

You wish for the end to your nightmarish dream

They call it life but it is not what it seems

<u>Clover</u>

I walk on the edge of a sharp knife

As I navigate my way through life

I live in a world were no one cares

No one sees me but everyone stares

Into the fire right out of the pan

Burned up heart no one understands

Start to go over but pull myself back

Right over the edge into a body sack

When it is all said and done and over

I know it would feel like rolling in clover

<u>The Chair I Passed Upon</u>

I sit vacantly alone in the dark in my chair

I hope that you are the one who finds me there

To see what has become of the pain that you gave

That built the path that led to my grave

Think about how many times that you made me cry

All of the times that you wished that I would die

Before you there was Sun and happiness all around

After you darkness and loneliness is my only sound

Striations of pain running ghostly through my brain

No thoughts of you will be buried with my remains

I expect no tears to fall or any flowers to be brought

As I pay for the destruction that you have wrought

By sitting vacantly alone in the dark in my chair

I hope that you are the one who finds me there

To see what has become of the pain that you gave

That built the path that led to my grave

<u>Suicidal</u>

People say that I am suicidal

Just because my emotions are tidal

I am happy next minute I am sad

See what I want and not what I have

Think you love me but I am not so sure

Not knowing is more than I can endure

Like waves crashing on a rocky shore

You give me all but I just need more

My smile is my frown I always wear

To hide the fact that no one cares

When my mind starts to become idle

I do start to feel suicidal

Contemplating

As I stand upon this chair

I realize I do not even care

This world is more than I can stand

So I hold this rope in my hand

Hide myself away from the Sun

In my hand I hold a loaded gun

Think about putting it to my head

Pulling the trigger until I am dead

Going to slice and slice until I bleed

No longer this pain inside do I need

Am going to use the point of this knife

This world is going to kill my life

Sitting alone in the dark contemplating

I am getting tired of all this waiting

Should I really do what I want to do

I just hope that in the end I am through

The Curse Of The Dead

I hear the thundering rumbling sound

Blood hits like heavy rain on the ground

Bodies are stacked like cords of wood

Results of the death of man's brotherhood

The scars left behind no one can see

It is all just a coming of destiny

Written in the stars like a book

Cannot read them if you never look

Scariness of looking to far ahead

A view point from the dead

<u>Echoes Of Your Love</u>

I hear the echoes of your love in my heart

Been there since the night we did part

They call out to me when I am feeling cold

Echos of love are something that you cannot hold

I can see right through the light into the dark

It takes everything I have and wrecks my heart

The echoes of your love try to save me but never will

I cannot be saved by something that is not real

Echoes of your love are not enough for me anymore

Why can we not love each other like we did before?

Echoes of your love cannot be all that it can be

No more echoes of your love for me

Echoes of your love call to me saying everything is fine

Echoes of your love through my heart and my mind

Echoes of your love follow me everywhere I go

Echoes of your love is now all I know

Expressive Decay

The fluidity of my life trickles on

Uncontrolled chaos arises like the dawn

I try my best to find a way to the top

Everywhere I look there is always a stop

People look but they do not want to see

They do not want to look at the reality of me

The cracks in the mirror always tells the truth

My last years are foretold by my youth

What I was is what I am and always will be

A living branch torn from a long dead tree

<u>Grip</u>

I take my hands and hold on tight

I know that one night I will fall

My grip is slowly loosening

I know soon that I will lose it all

People can be so phony with a smile

Like they are rehearsing their lines

For a movie that is never meant to be seen

One that only plays inside their minds

My reality is dissolving into a blur

Of a fictitious coloring scheme

The grip on my mind is dubious

Light into darkness is my nightmares dream

Worst Color Of Blue

You love her but she does not love you

That is the worst color of blue

Your heart aches, you cry all the time

Unrequited love is the worst kind

You want her but you know you cannot

It hurts wanting what you have not got

Her body is inviting, her mind just will not go

All the love you have for her you cannot show

You go through life alone only loving her

No other alive can make your heart stir

You try but there is nothing you can do

That is the worst color of blue

The Storm

When we held each other in arms

I fell for her seductive charms

She is my oasis in a lonely night

I am quenched when I hold her tight

Comes the storm to blow it all away

Like a house of cards we fell that day

She loved another that was not me

My tears flowed out like a dead sea

Take my story right into your heart

Or your world will be broken apart

Prepare yourself for when it is done

One day the storm is going to come

<u>Skin</u>

My covering is too thick to penetrate

I hide my broken heart with hate

I love you but you do not love me

I want you to stay but you leave

You could mend my broken heart

Put it back together like the very start

My skin is a suit of armor I hide inside

I say I do not love you, once again I lied

My skin has become hard over the pain

When all is gone my skin will still remain

<u>Casualty Of War</u>

Awoke by the distant sounds of the drums of war

Want me to take the lives of people I never seen before

They tell me that they are the enemy so they must die

I am sure they are telling the other side the same lie

I find myself buried in a faraway muddy foxhole

Encircled by darkness as the cannons smoke blows

I write a blood soaked letter to send to no one at all

As bullets fly by me those around me start to fall

I know that I will soon die like so many have before

To be marked down simply as a casualty of war

I Call It Home

I have been gone away for so long

The world is cold when you are all alone

I just want to go back home and stay

Have cried the whole time I been away

It will be so warm and peaceful there

No more pain or sorrow or even a care

No more dark skies will be over my head

Love will be meant whenever it is said

Hope that you welcome me with open arms

Hope you hug and hold me take away my harms

Will be smiling with joy deep within my eyes

The day that I go home to brighter skies

Ghost In The Crowd

Standing in the rain waiting for the Sun

Looking for a rainbow that never comes

Search for a silver lining that can never be

Hidden by dark clouds that hang over me

Words like daggers digging into my soul

Buried deeper and deeper as they flow

Feel like a boat pitching on a raging sea

Crashing waves of pain washing over me

Grasp for love but there is none to be found

I know that I am surely going to drown

Walking around cold on a hot summer day

No crowd can keep the loneliness away

I am like a ghost that can never be seen

Not loved or hated just somewhere in between

<u>**Invisible Hands**</u>

Invisible hands push me toward the ledge

Hidden shadows behind a foreboding hedge

Jumped or pushed what difference does it make

All pain known recedes within the final wake

Dragged through the mud of someone others desire

Shaking and quaking me onto the funeral pyre

Invisible hands trap me by the throat tightly

Pulls me into my dreams from reality nightly

Terrors real more than unreal flying in my head

They see me as better off if I am dead

<u>Schiz</u>

There are two people who live inside

For one to live the other must die

They struggle and fight in my mind

I am stuck in the middle all of the time

One tries to tell me what I should do

The other says that it is just not true

I have tried to push them both aside

Sometimes they just refuse to hide

When one side buries the other deep

Into my life it does slowly start to creep

Try to push them both to where they belong

But they will not stay there for very long

There are two people who live inside

For one to live the other must die

<u>Crash</u>

I am headed for a terrible crash

No way I will be coming back

Leaving here just as fast as I can

Cannot stay where I cannot stand

Can no longer face this cruel reality

It is starting to take its toll on me

I am about to hit head on a wall

Can hear the echo of the graves call

I am headed for a terrible crash

I will stay and I will never come back

<u>Slip</u>

Slip, slipping away

Trying to find a better way

The pain inside is so hard to hide

As deeper into depression I do slide

She took her love away from me

She decided that is how it must be

I have decided that I just do not belong

Living in this world that feels so wrong

I feel like I am dead on a string

I can no longer feel anything

Frequent flier miles from Hell

Reality is starting to penetrate my shell

Let me take you on a tour inside

Underneath the places that I hide

Lied to you and to myself

Nothing of me is left

Shrink

Shrink me down to a cell

Lock me away in your jail

I can never again be free

I can never again be me

Something just put away

Out of sight out of the way

Locked inside of darkness

Thought of less and less

No longer remembered anymore

Forgotten thought forevermore

<u>The Truth?</u>

What do you do when the truth turns out to be a lie

When you have no one else on which you can rely

When all you friends turn out to be fake

Everything you knew you have to forsake

When everything you thought is wrong

You have nowhere left that you belong

Lost in the dark for years and years

You finally see where the light does peer

Find the truth that was carefully hidden

By the ones who use you to do there bidding

<u>Shade</u>

I live in the shadow of your cold shade

Frozen in place by past mistakes I have made

Seismic echoes of pain running through my veins

In my cryptic blood it flows now I must drain

When I love it always ends up the same

In the end I am the only one left to blame

In the shade of the mirror truth must be told

In the shade I am the only one left for me to hold

I try to hide away from the things that I have done

Inside of the shadows of the shade away from the Sun

<u>Insanium</u>

There are fractures appearing in my cranium

Voices are saying I am becoming more insanium

Hearing things that I do not see anymore

Monsters clawing inside my walls more and more

My life is just like a decaying old geranium

People are saying I am becoming derangium

Laughing through their pretentious concern

As my mind flickers away into ashes of burn

I wish I had a skin that was made of titanium

Their painful word arrows are driving me insanium

They pierce my very soul drain my blood like a knife

I am slowly losing my mind and taking away my life

I am being taken away by small doses of radium

When I am finally gone from this hurtful saniumn

Will anyone care I have moved to a different plane

On to a place where insane is really to be sane

<u>**In Memoriam Of My Mom**</u>

<u>**(Passed July 7th 2012)**</u>

In your loving memory

I shed my tears for thee

Whenever you were near

I was glad you were here

For the life that you gave me

I could never repay thee

Each tear that does fall

Is another memory I recall

When I come to visit you

There is nothing I can do

Except to cry a shower

As I cover you with flowers

In your loving memory

I shed my tears for thee

Wishing you were still here

To dry my petrified tears